Praise

"Angie Athanassiades uses language with the precision of a sculptor wielding a chisel, patiently chipping away hardened layers of trauma to free the clean-limbed life that has been buried inside the rough stone. Fiercely beautiful, this 'memoir in fragments' cracks open the darkness and pain of sexual assault to reveal light, hope and a sense of freedom."
SAMANTHA CLARK, AUTHOR OF *THE CLEARING*

"Set on the remote island of Antikythera in the Aegean Sea, this haunting memoir by Angie Athanassiades reveals how the island became her sanctuary; and how the sea, the migrating birds, and the alchemy of time helped her heal from long-ago trauma. Lovely and lyrical, this book is a treasure."
CLARE MACQUEEN, FOUNDING EDITOR AND PUBLISHER OF *MACQUEEN'S QUINTERLY*

"Angie Athanassiades's writing is clear and precise, beautiful in the way it conveys the natural world and honest in how it renders a person moving forward after assault. There is pain here, and joy, and wings that feel real."
CAITLIN JANS, CO-FOUNDER OF *AUTHORS PUBLISH MAGAZINE*

"How to honor this work with the deepest respect and gladness? Poet Angie Athanassiades offers us as readers an elemental healing gift. We have the chance to reclaim our bodies as she makes whole her own again, an act of sacred alchemy. The stark beauty and simplicity of her prose evokes comparison with Terry Tempest Williams. She fully dances with nature as she faces harsh realities and transforms into the next moment. She finds her own way back to a new place of safety with the birds of Antikythera in the Aegean Sea. So very glad I read this!"
AMADEA MORNINGSTAR, AUTHOR OF *BREATHE FREE*

"A lucid, unsentimental, and quietly beautiful collection. *I Am Twig, Bone, Feather* is a fittingly elemental title for a work that questions what shapes us, what makes us a person. I read it straight through."
BEA SETTON, AUTHOR OF *BERLIN*

About the Author

Angie Athanassiades is a British/Greek memoirist, poet, essayist and teacher. Her writing is inspired by nature, mythology and art. Her essays have appeared in publications such as *KYSO Flash and Serving House Journal*, and have been nominated for the Pushcart Prize and the Best of the Net award, while her most recent poem, "Heather," was published in Linen Press's anthology *Look Away Now*. She currently lives in Greece where she loves to walk with her dog in the forest and on the island of Antikythera, collecting twigs, bones and feathers, and watching migrating birds.

twigbonefeather.com

I am Twig Bone Feather

ANGIE ATHANASSIADES

I Am Twig, Bone, Feather

Print Edition
ISBN: 978-3-98832-214-2
Published by Vine Leaves Press 2026

Cover design by Jessica Bell
Interior design by Amie McCracken

Photos in Fragments 57, 59, and 63 have been reproduced with the permission of the Photographic Agency of the Musée Rodin, Paris, France.

Fragment 57, Title: The Swimmer, Author: Auguste Rodin, Inventory No.: D.3992, Media: Woven paper | Graphite pencil | Watercolor, Dimensions: H. 25.1 cm; W. 33 cm, Photo credit: Photo credit: © Musée Rodin, photo Jean de Calan, Provenance: Musée Rodin

Fragment 59, Title: Shipwreck, Author: Auguste Rodin, Inventory No.: D.4081, Medium: vellum paper | graphite pencil | watercolor, Dimensions: H. 25 cm; W. 32.3 cm, Photo credit: © Musée Rodin, photo Jean de Calan, Provenance: Musée Rodin

Fragment 63, Title: Nude Woman in Profile with Loose Hair, Author: Auguste Rodin, Inventory No.: D.5014, Media: Woven paper | Graphite pencil | Stump | Watercolor, Dimensions: H. 32.2 cm; W. 24 cm, Photo credit: Photo credit: © Musée Rodin, photo Jean de Calan, Provenance: Musée Rodin

For Pericles & Marina,
and for the honey buzzards of Antikythera
who showed me the way home.

Proem

When I used to try to remember and panicked, I would cover my eyes and press on them until they hurt. But now I've discovered that placing my palms firmly between my navel and my pubic bone, covering and gently pressing down on my uterus, makes me feel contained, safer, stronger.

My navel, where my root once grew from; where my root, my cord, was cut at birth. We are all, then, rootless.

My navel, the centre of my body, of my world, my omphalos.

Omphalos, the Greek word for navel and the sacred stone at Delphi, believed to have been the centre of the universe; kept in the adyton, the space not to be entered.

I am my own oracle, pilgrim and priestess. I contain both the question and the riddle.

I.

Fragment 1

If I were a bird, I would be a vagrant, an accidental,

one that has strayed, or has been blown off its usual migratory route.

Fragment 2
Island of Antikythera

I look around the strange, well-like harbour. The boat is almost gone already, wasting no time on its way to Crete, leaving nothing behind it but roiled water, a shimmering trail of reflected light, and me, standing on the quay I looked at for months in a photo I found online and pinned to the wall of my study.

Fragment 3

I am lying in my bunk, listening to the sounds of night in this unfamiliar place, waiting for the dawn. I have been awake for hours, quite still, wondering at the incredible blackness of the dark, more doubtful as time wears on that dawn will ever have the strength to break through it.

Fragment 4

The island is as remote as they say.

From the ledge where I sit the next morning outside the guesthouse, all I can see are treeless slopes, the sea, its surface flexing to meet the wind, dappled as the light of the sun finds its way through white clouds onto the ruckled surface; and the sky, everywhere, massive, drawing the gaze up, up, and away, over a horizon ethereal, but alive with the promise of travelling birds.

The white owl I heard in the black darkness is now sleeping. The little snake that disappeared into the dark bush like a startled ribbon is now sleeping.

Fragment 5

There is no path leading to the ruined windmill, just a steep slope covered in thorny shrubs. The roof and most of the wall have collapsed. The large stones that were once used to build it are now heaped inside and around it as though they all tumbled down at the same time.

Some of the beams that once made up the wooden parts are lying amongst the stones, most of them broken and rotting, but in some of the pieces it is still possible to see that they'd been part of a mechanism: a perfect indent, a hole with rust around its edges.

The wind has dropped, but even the light breeze makes the shattered windmill appear a tragic figure, its once-powerful blades which had generated energy to feed the island now lying broken, still and powerless in the wind, amongst the stones that had once held them firm.

I lay my palm on one of the wooden pieces, hoping it might reveal something of its past, but feel only dampness.

But when I bend down to smell the black wood, it smells of earth and mould. This wood has died two deaths: first when it was cut down as a tree in some faraway place, then here, when the windmill stopped being used.

Now it is lying amongst the soil and rubble, already on a new journey, the fungi and bacteria busy at work to help it return to the earth.

It will take time, but of that there is plenty here.

Fragment 6

When the falcons appear, they startle me with their shrill calls, and I watch as they play with each other, soaring, diving, looping.

I reach the top of the slope, expecting a ridge, but discover a long, narrow plateau. Its edge runs along the south-eastern side of the island, a sheer drop down to the sea. I take a few steps back, my legs unsteady from the pull of the drop, and I look out towards the horizon.

To the south I can see the north-western part of Crete.

To the east there is nothing but sea, a bright cobalt in the late morning sun, and a sky that looks like it's melting into the water, making it bluer still as it dissolves into it.

Fragment 7

I walk. I walk along the one road, I walk on paths cleared by wild goats, on paths cleared years ago by people who are now too old to walk them any longer; who had known them like the marks on their bodies, but can now only tell me where they lead.

I walk. I walk looking up and around me, at the sea and sky
—so much blue—

and when it all becomes too much, when it becomes unbearable
—so much freedom—

I turn away and look at the ground.

I find shards of ancient pottery, strewn amongst the shrubs of thyme and heather, find twigs and branches of juniper, twisted, bent, like dry muscle. I find bones of goats and birds, scattered pell-mell by wind and rain. I find feathers, shed by falcons and barn owls, kestrels, and ravens.

So I begin to gather. I gather wind-bent wood, battered feathers, bones smooth as cowrie shells. I fill my backpack, my pockets, my notebook.

Every day I gather more and lay them on a shelf in the room where I sleep.

Fragment 8

The passerines arrive first,
indiscernible, almost invisible.

a slight quivering of the shrubs,
a flash of colour,
then another:

blue
grey
yellow

a song
a trill

fine threads of colour and sound
weaving a dazzling tapestry of arrival.

Elated by their seeming weightlessness,
I feel despondent when I find them flightless in the road,
their bodies heavy with exhaustion,
with the effort of continuous flight,

so much like my own.

Fragment 9

I feel my body change on the island.

Endless hours of walking, of moving in the white heat of day, in the darkling blue of evening, in the stillness of the night.

It is becoming leaner, lighter, stronger, the muscles beneath the skin growing firmer, longer.

My body is coming into its own.

And I am letting it, letting it breathe again,

letting it feel,

and it feels nourished, alive. Even as it sleeps, still warm from the day's heat in the cool darkness.

In this landscape, with its handful of houses and even fewer people, with its seemingly endless expanses of land, sea, and sky, I feel safe, free;

my body feels free for the first time ever.

Fragment 10

I can feel every inch of my skin when I shower in the evenings, adjusting the water from hot to cold, feeling for my skin's response, learning what soothes, hurts, or surprises it.

I look at sections of skin, darker by the day, as I dry myself, rub cream into it cautiously, as though touching a new lover, curious to see how it will respond.

I trace the fresh scars of cuts and grazes with my fingertips, notice how the same scar feels different at the tip of each finger. I watch my muscles tense and relax under my skin as I move to dress, feel my body react, respond, adjust.

Each night I go to bed a little different, my body and I a little more familiar, sinking together into a dreamless sleep in a darkness thick and heavy with silence.

Every morning, I wake up just before dawn, in that half hour when the whole world seems to be holding its breath.

My grandmother's shawl loosely flung over my shoulders, I make myself a cup of tea and drink it on the spot on the patio where I sat that first morning and watch as another dawn burns and bleeds into the sky. Every morning the same ritual. Every morning a different sky. Every morning a slightly different me. Sore muscles, sweet exhaustion, and a horizon quivering with promise.

I am finding my way back to a long-lost me, one tired, bewildered step at a time.

Fragment 11

(I look at my hands, my body, and imagine that under all that skin and flesh my skeleton is an intricate construction made of wood, my phalanges delicate twigs, my tibiae and humeri long, smooth branches, my sacrum and cranium water-sculpted driftwood, my patellae tree knots.

The Ancient Greek word for wood was also the word for primordial matter, *hyle.*

Maybe someday, out of the gathered wood and bones and feathers, I will create a creature motley and wild, part bird, part human, part animal, and will name it 'hyle,' or 'so this is me, then.')

Fragment 12

Just off the north-eastern tip of the island, three rocks emerge from the sea.

They're called *Thimonies,* the Greek word for bales, as in bales of hay, or wheat, recalling, like the windmill, the days when the island was alive with fertile fields and with people tending them.

Just off these rocks, in 1900, wearing a canvas suit and copper helmet, sponge diver Elias Stadiatis descended to a depth of forty-five metres, only to discover what he thought was a heap of rotting corpses of humans and horses strewn amongst the rocks and silt of the sea floor. He had, in fact, discovered an ancient shipwreck and, among the findings, were human bones.

Since then, three different expeditions have come to the island in the hope of discovering and retrieving more remains.

Fragment 13

Over time, and by countless different hands, bones, bronze and marble limbs and bodies, glass cups and bowls, were pulled out of the dark water, brought to the surface, and carried to spaces very different, dry, light, sterile, to be analysed, identified, named.

In one of those spaces, the bones were washed, dried, and prepared for examination. After analysing features of the cranial morphology, and in particular, the glabella, supraorbital ridges, and nuchal crest,[1] it was determined that the best-preserved skull, almost entire, had belonged to a young woman.

We are made of water, of carbon, of air,

contain rivers, caves, ridges, and crests

we are our own landscapes

Fragment 14

A vagrant bird, an accidental, blown off course.

Was she returning home, or travelling to a new one?

Did she see the outline of the island's ridges, the ragged coastline—a stone's throw away—before the sea rushed into the branching limbs of her lungs? Did she believe that she might survive? Or did she realise, in those last moments, that this would be her final home?

Fragment 15

As I sit perched on a hill overlooking the sea, sheltered from sun and wind by the ruined walls of an ancient fort, I watch as divers and marine archaeologists arrive in their boats and drop anchor just south of Thimonies, over the site of the shipwreck.

No sooner have the divers climbed into their wetsuits than the wind picks up, churning the darkening water, tossing the boats about.

The divers climb out of their wetsuits, the anchors are pulled, the boats leave to return to the safety of the harbour.

It will be the first of many attempts.

Fragment 16

I watch the divers wait for days for the wind to settle,

the sea to still.

I watch their boats, tiny against the massive blue, so easily tossed and thrown about, toys in a bathtub.

Even when the surface calms, the water beneath is pushed and pulled by forceful currents.

The conditions need to be safe, just so, for the work to begin.

Fragment 17

And then one day, everything stands still, at just the right time, and, with a heave and a splash, in and down they go, into the blue, into the darker blue, into the past.

I wish I could dive in with them, follow them down, swim over the sloping shelf the wreck was found on, over marble limbs lying silently amongst sponges and anemones;

in search of the past,

my own,

here, on this island, where everything is safe, where everything is just so.

Fragment 18

But memory rarely complies with our need
to attach experience to metaphor;
she is her own master,
finding her cues in her own good time,
in scents, sounds, images,
we ourselves are slow to recognize
even as we look at the real
world around us.

Fragment 19

Something inside me is distracting me, making me restless,

like a word hovering on the tip of my tongue.

I leave the divers to their work—I will not find any answers there—and look around me, for days, desperate to find the elusive thing—whatever it may be—that will coax that something to the surface.

I know it is the reason I am here, but trying to think it into something real, something I can see in my mind, is like trying to capture the invisible.

I leave it, give it space, hoping if I ignore it, it will reveal itself.

So I turn to the sky.

Fragment 20

I wouldn't hope to touch the sky with both arms.

— Sappho

Fragment 21

For days nothing happens.

Until one morning, just after dawn, the sky's texture changes as a chill north wind begins to blow over the island and the surrounding water.

Tiny white clouds, fine as down, appear in the bluer, brighter sky, but rather than gather, they string together like daisy chains and rush across the sky towards the south.

Pulled and lifted by the same wind, the sea's surface starts to stir, forming its own white clouds of foam on the crests of southbound waves.

It's the *meltemi*.

Fragment 22

Every August, high-pressure systems over the Balkans meet low-pressure systems forming over Turkey, creating a powerful Etesian wind known in Greek as 'meltemi.'

Although many believe the name is a loan from the Italian 'mal tempo,' meaning 'bad weather,' according to the ancient lexicographer Hesychius of Alexandria, it derives from the Greek 'melissemein,' meaning to soothe, to console.

These winds, also known as *katabatic,* descending, bring to the eastern Mediterranean much-needed coolness, but also serve as flyways for migrating raptors travelling from the Balkan forests to Africa.

Fragment 23

When the raptors begin to arrive,
they are powerful, determined,
their flight driven by intent,
by the call of destination.

How do they manage,
I wonder,
this suspended existence,
this life of two homes,
of two separate truths,

a life of no winters?

I envy them,
ground-bound as I am,
weighed down by story,

and watch them
as they fly above me,
hoping their flight might
teach me how to leave
a dark and heavy past
behind me.

Fragment 24

As though some universal signal were given, undetectable to human ears, the birds begin to arrive in large—some days unfathomable—numbers.

The morning skies are empty but charged with anticipation, the nights a long, tense pause between arrivals and departures.

It is all about temperature, of course, pure physics, as birds need the thermals that form around land masses during the warmer times of day to glide rather than fly, preserving their precious energy, but to me it feels like some primal magic is at work.

Fragment 25

When the honey buzzards arrive, I am not prepared for it.

I have been walking all day, my body is tired, my mind blown empty from the north wind that has been blasting since morning.

But as I sit on the ledge outside the guesthouse looking at the horizon, I notice a darkening of the sky, a swathe of grey, uneven, speckled, as though painted by the fevered brush of an Impressionist.

I stand up to get my binoculars, but there is no time. Within seconds, it seems, they are approaching, hundreds of them, just feet away from me.

Anxious to see it all, see them all, I lie on the ground and watch as they pass above me, white, black, brown, cream, brown, black, brown, white; so close I can count their primaries, can see their talons furled for flight, can see their talons press against their bodies by the sheer force of it. Some look young, taut, others older, battered, worn.

Every now and again, one will fly close enough to cast a weightless shadow over me, and, for a fleeting moment, it feels like the sky is touching me, like I too am flying.

Fragment 26

Meltemi, from the same root as 'meli,' meaning 'honey.'

Fragment 27

When solitary birds arrive, alone in the late morning or early evening sky, they look like omens, harbingers, heralds of the gods.

Standing in a landscape where past and present are barely visible in fragile fragments that only tell part of a story—a house here, an ancient ruin there—time becomes larger, expanding into one all-encompassing space, free from the confines of chronology.

At times I feel like a seer, an apprentice prophet trying to learn the language of augury.

I think back to the stories that informed my imagination as a child, as a young woman; to Homer, to Euripides and Ovid; to birds as messengers, as vehicles of disguise, of redemption.

I think of Priam, Hector's father, how when he saw an eagle flying through the city of Troy, his grieving heart grew hopeful for he knew his prayers to Zeus had been answered, that his request to ransom his son's body back from the Greeks would be granted.

I think of Penelope, distrustful of the Gods, trusting not the birds she saw in the sky, but those appearing in her own dreams as she slept.

I think of Philomela, ravaged and mutilated into eternal silence, transformed into a nightingale, singing at dawn.

I think of Leda.

Fragment 28

"Jupiter, changed into a swan, had intercourse with Leda near the River Eurotas, and from that embrace she bore Pollux and Helen."[2]

Fragment 29

I imagine her swimming in the river when the swan
approaches, vulnerable out of her element.

Charmed by the wild creature, so beautiful, so close, she
smiles, extending a dripping arm towards it.

But sensing something unnatural in the singularity of its
intent,

she retreats, her feet treading water
as he glides ever closer;

and in a beat of wings, a plash of water,

he is upon her.

Fragment 30

What colour is pain?

What colour is my pain?

Fragment 31

I think of my layers of pain as wax, my body an encaustic artwork.

In encaustic painting, heated wax, usually mixed with pigment, is applied to a surface—prepared wood, canvas, or other materials. As the applied wax cools and hardens, more layers can be added. By scraping or reheating and melting the surface, different layers are revealed. When unpigmented wax is also used, it can lend a translucent aspect to the surface, a kind of membrane, or skin.

The term is derived from ancient Greek, meaning 'to burn in.'

I am curious about the process, intrigued by how much the layers resemble trauma becoming part of and residing in the body; how depending on which parts we scrape or melt away, different memories of pain can be brought to the surface once again.

I imagine recreating my body on a sheet of prepared wood, layer upon layer, the first one dark, a maroon mixed by Rothko, the next one lighter, and so on, until the final one is unpigmented, almost clear.

I imagine working on the area between my navel and my pubic bone, melting the layers away, revealing the ever-darkening colours until the maroon appears, a wound, a core of pain still raw.

Fragment 32

As the title suggests, encaustic artist Tony Scherman is unambiguous about the nature of the encounter in his collection entitled 'The Rape of Leda.'

The collection comprises nineteen images.

There are two of Jupiter as swan, one beautiful, graceful, set against a light background; the other, set against black, sinister, threatening.

Cerberus, curious and alert, his black and white coat ruffled by the wind as he perches attentively on the top of a slope.

Persephone, dark, seductive, a black net veiling covering her black-rimmed eyes.

Diana, as a stag, looking directly ahead.

Minerva, lush lips, turban, set against an orange backdrop that resembles the heat of fire.

Boadicea, looking on, remembering her daughters.

They are the silent witnesses.

There are roses, some gathered from Cicero's Garden, some representing The Coming Good, betokening eventual relief. They speak of innocence and beauty, but also of the desire to take, to have, regardless.

There is no image of Leda.

Fragment 33

The absence of Leda from the collection says more than any image could convey.

Surprising at first, her absence makes me think of:

the fact that when that kind of trauma occurs, there is a departure, an absence that is vital to survival. The cognitive brain shutting down. Not being there.

The fact that if we assume the series of paintings is her recollection of the event, memories of traumatic experiences are fragmented, at best; do not adhere to a linear, logical sequence.

The fact that her absence speaks of the dismissal of her version of the events.

She has no voice. As victim, her account of the event does not matter. Her experience is not her own.

Leda is not there. Her voice, her experience, are not there.

Fragment 34

I swim, try to feel every sensation, how my body responds submerged in the cool sea-water. I am tense at first, and try relaxing my body, letting it rise to the surface.
I feel my skin as one entire, finite thing; one organ, indeed, every inch touched by water. But when my body rises to the surface and my limbs move apart and away from my core, I feel exposed, vulnerable, unable to protect myself.
The feeling so familiar, sickening, I swim to shallow water and crouch wrapping my arms around my knees, a foetus, rocking in lapping, liquid blue light.

(salt water, a body of tears)

amniotic fluid, from the Greek *amnos*, meaning 'lamb'

Fragment 35

I learned two words yesterday: vena, which 'vein' comes from and means a small underground channel of water, and the verb 'to craze,' which means to produce a fine network of cracks on a surface.

I can relate to both.

Every now and then, when I think words have failed me, when I think they cannot begin to describe what I lived through and how it changed me, they appear, in all their tiny, linear shapes. They're all I have; I have words.

Fragment 36

When the body freezes or submits, when it realises it can neither fight nor flee, the cognitive brain shuts down. When you freeze, terrified because you are immobilised, the part of your brain that can reason, that can explain what is happening with logic and language, shuts down. Everything from there on is experienced and recorded by the right brain as a visceral and emotional memory.

This is why people who have experienced trauma during which they couldn't fight or flee often find it impossible to describe the event using language. They try writing about what happened or talking about it, but none of it seems real. None of it accurately describes what really happened, how it actually felt.

So I find myself searching for words. Writing it up, as it happened, minute by minute, I read it back and it reads like a stranger's story. I read it and see the events that happened, but I can't describe the fear, the pain, the terrifying helplessness.

The distance too great between the reality and the words failing to describe it.

Fragment 37

Varying degrees of intimacy and violence in the different phrasing.
Concerns about those reading it.

violation
sexual assault
rape victim
I was sexually assaulted
I was raped

Where does the difference lie?

Fragment 38

Writing about rape is hard in a different way than I expected. I didn't realise it would test my relationship to language, make me think about the connection and difference between truth and acceptable fact.

I have the words 'rape' and 'violation' and 'assault.' But I want to use the words 'pain' and 'swelling' and 'torn.' I want to use 'disgusting,' 'revolting,' and 'rotting'. I want people to know that rape is awful, repulsive. I want people to know that rape makes you not want to touch yourself. It makes you live in a body you are disgusted by. It makes you a stranger in the one thing you thought was your own.

Fragment 39

I know I can say 'now, finally, I can talk about it. Now I feel that a certain degree of healing might be possible.'

Perhaps I could even say 'now I no longer hate my body; now, finally, I want to turn inward, slip inside myself and comfort that part of me that was hurt so badly.'

But does anybody want to know the painful, disgusting details? The details that sicken and repulse?

Can I say 'walking home the morning after, I could feel something seeping out of me, trickling down my bruised, shaking legs, and thought 'please, let it be blood?'

Can I say 'my body disgusted me?'

Can I say 'I tried to wash him out of me, but touching the swollen, torn lips of my vagina was too painful?'

Fragment 40

I could write a thousand descriptions, but what I remember
is
the stench of his sweat on my skin as I walked home the
next morning
the torn skin on all my lips
that it hurt like hell
that I tried not to drink for as long as I could because I was
terrified of peeing

Fragment 41

I split in two that night.
Half of me felt disgusting, repulsive, pathetic—
the other half terrified; terrified and voiceless.

Fragment 42

My body broke.
My body betrayed me.

(this could, would, never be undone)

Fragment 43

(I found a wing once; a single, entire gull wing. It looked so perfect, so whole.

A riven limb of a phantom body.)

Fragment 44

I was wearing an ankle-length purple skirt, a black ribbed vest, a red and black shisha waistcoat with tiny mirrors stitched into the fabric, battered blue Doc Martens.

I never wore these clothes again, apart from the waistcoat. It had been a gift from my grandmother. I wore it at a party, years later, and felt like I was asking for it, in my mirrored waistcoat, baggy jeans, and Birkenstocks.

I kept the skirt, vest, and Doc Martens in a black bin bag in a wardrobe; evidence, memento, token of shame, of pain. Until I threw the bag in a dumpster and waited so I could watch the truck take it away.

For years I kept the waistcoat in an old suitcase, where I put clothes for safekeeping; my memories of my grandmother folded away with my memories of the rape.

Fragment 45

Fuck forgiveness
I want to hear him scream
watch him bruise and bleed
until there is nothing left of him

Fragment 46

Petrous Bone: The dense, rock-like part of the temporal bone that contains the inner ear, located at the base of the skull.

Named after its density, from the Greek *petra,* meaning stone, the tiny, wing-shaped petrous bone has been found to preserve DNA better than any other part of the skeleton or the teeth.

A wing near a cave where sounds are heard. Where silence, too, is heard.

Fragment 47

There is a silence that comes with pain internalised, pain refused, pain rejected by the body; by the rational and emotional self. A pain that shame and incomprehension make intolerable. But the body is a curious creature, with countless systems working independently of others.

Sometimes, while parts of the body reject an event because it is too painful to process, other parts, parts that understand survival differently, break the silence, override the rejection and continue, regardless.

Fragment 48

and amongst the hyacinths, Leda found

an egg hidden

— Sappho

Fragment 49

Medical termination of pregnancy.[3]

(1) Subject to the provisions of this section, a person shall not be guilty of an offence under the law relating to abortion when a pregnancy is terminated by a registered medical practitioner if two registered medical practitioners are of the opinion, formed in good faith—

(a) that the pregnancy has not exceeded its twenty-fourth week and that the continuance of the pregnancy would involve risk, greater than if the pregnancy were terminated, of injury to the physical or mental health of the pregnant woman or any existing children of her family; or

(b) that the termination is necessary to prevent grave permanent injury to the physical or mental health of the pregnant woman; or

(c) that the continuance of the pregnancy would involve risk to the life of the pregnant woman, greater than if the pregnancy were terminated; or

(d) that there is a substantial risk that if the child were born it would suffer from such physical or mental abnormalities as to be seriously handicapped.

Fragment 50

'Yes,' I said to the medical counsellor when she asked if I was certain I wanted to terminate the pregnancy. 'It was rape.'

'You were raped?' she asked, looking alarmed.

'Yes, I was raped.'

It was the first time I said it out loud, and the last time I would say it for a long time.

She wrote something down and I imagined she was checking 'b' on the form.

She continued to talk in a tone that was softer, kinder, but I was no longer listening, had returned to my silence.

Fragment 51

This silence was different. Deafening, hollow.

It was the silence of betrayal answered with betrayal;

my body, me, and I, in turn, my body.

There could be no healing after this.

Fragment 52

As the memories return, I wonder why they chose this island to do so, but the longer I stay, the clearer it becomes:

the landscape bare, seemingly stripped of narrative and context, but strewn with the remains of silenced stories;

the birds, continuously arriving and departing, driven by the primal instinct to survive, no matter what;

the boundless sea and sky inviting thoughts of hope, of deliverance.

II.

II

Fragment 53
Athens,
Temple of Artemis, Vravrona

Autumn

In a wetland near the eastern coast of Attica, amongst tamarisks, reeds, and bullrush, the Temple of Artemis stands, quite softly, in the brackish earth.

It is a beautiful spot, close to the city, but peaceful, sheltered by a wreath of green hills, and while the sea is not visible from the temple's grounds, the air smells of the Aegean.

At this temple, over two thousand years ago, young girls would gather to bring votive offerings to Artemis, the protectress of unmarried girls.

Dressed as bears and carrying baskets of figs, some would perform ritual dances, marking their menarche, the first stage of early womanhood. Others, older, danced to mark their arrival at the age of marriage. The younger ones brought offerings of toys made of bone, or little clay sculptures of bears, bulls, and lambs, while the older girls brought bone or ivory combs and mirrors.

Fragment 54

I am no longer a young girl, and have no clay animals to offer nor combs made of bone. I have come bearing nothing but the fragments of my story;

hoping
this peaceful place, this sacred space, might offer me sanctuary;

hoping
that the goddess might grant me the grace I need to begin putting my pieces back together.

But as I come to the end of the path that leads to the grounds, I find the gate locked. I can see the temple through the fence, submerged in water from recent floods.

It looks as though it's floating, its reflection in the water shimmering in the morning light.

I watch from afar, as herons feed among the reeds and sparrows land and perch on the temple's columns.

Away from the island, forbidden from entering the temple, I have no recourse but to create my own space of safety, find a different kind of grace.

If only I could fly.

Fragment 55

In a series of drawings by Auguste Rodin, female figures drawn in graphite appear in different postures—crouched, reclining, standing.

In some of the drawings the posture is such that parts of the body are concealed, making the figure appear partial or dismembered.

There is no violence in this, however, as the drawings are painted over with a blue watercolour wash, removing the anticipated tension of violence, creating, rather, one of movement, of immersion and gradual surrender.

The blue wash was always added after the drawing was completed, the figure immersed in a context, an environment that is dynamic, narrative, transformative.

Fragment 56

I have my first panic attack whilst driving. The second outside my therapist's office, when she opens the door to meet me for the first time.

Fragment 57
The Swimmer

Autumn

In the drawing entitled *The Swimmer*, the female figure is in profile on all fours, the blue wash drawn in horizontal lines across the page creating a sense of force.

One of the figure's arms is bent and reaching forward, giving the impression that she is swimming, or trying to, against a powerful current.

Her face is distorted, her mouth open, in effort, pain, anger.

Her hair is brown, dark next to the pale skin tones of her body, as though she has yet to relinquish the implications of her temporality, is reluctant to leave the linear narrative from which she has been removed

Fragment 58

When the sessions begin, I start to think I will not be able to do it.

Every time the conversation moves closer to that night, my heart races, my hands begin to tremble; I feel sick, can't breathe.

When I try to push through, desperate to see it so that I can transform it with reason and words into something I can understand, desperate to reclaim language, my body reacts violently, heaves with sudden waves of grief and fear.

Fragment 59
Shipwreck

Winter

In the drawing entitled *Shipwreck*, a female figure is drawn in a reclined position, her head leaning back, her arms stretched above her head, the left hand grasping the right elbow. Her thighs are closed, her calves opening below the knees.

She is facing the viewer at an angle and her placement in the centre-left of the image creates a sense of space, of ease.

Horizontal lines drawn in graphite under her thighs and buttocks add gravity, stability, contrasting the movement and tension created by the curved lines resembling waves surrounding her.

She is at once safe and vulnerable.

If one looks closely, her facial expression, drawn in a few

faint, almost indiscernible, lines conveys relief.

It is hard to reconcile this seemingly peaceful image with the violence implied by the title, unless one notices a detail so subtle it is almost unbearable:

her feet are ever so slightly pointing downward, gently hanging.
There is nothing solid beneath her.

She is not languidly reclining—

she is being swept away
by shell-shaped waves.

The marks on her clothing—water dropped onto the watercolour—make her seem as though she is slowly becoming part of the water

she is being consumed

Fragment 60

I'm having night terrors and nightmares.

I feel as though I am constantly being thrown about by an unrelenting force, can find nothing solid to hold on to.

I am being consumed by the fear, the anger that's coming to the surface, by the terrifying realization of what I've been holding inside me for so long.

I look at the drawings. If only I could paint over everything with a soft blue wash, draw the beginning where I want.

Fragment 61

(I dreamed one night that my vagina
was a mouth with retractable teeth
hidden behind the lips, like a shark's.
That's the kind of vagina I want.
Those are the lips I'd kiss with.)

Fragment 62

I turn to the island, to metaphor.

I imagine I am a diver, diving into a dark blue, searching
here, there, in spaces ever darker;

and slowly,

hesitantly,

I begin to find one,

then another,

moments images

memories

some heavy as marble,

others fragile as ancient glass.

Fragment 63
Female Nude in Profile with Loose Hair

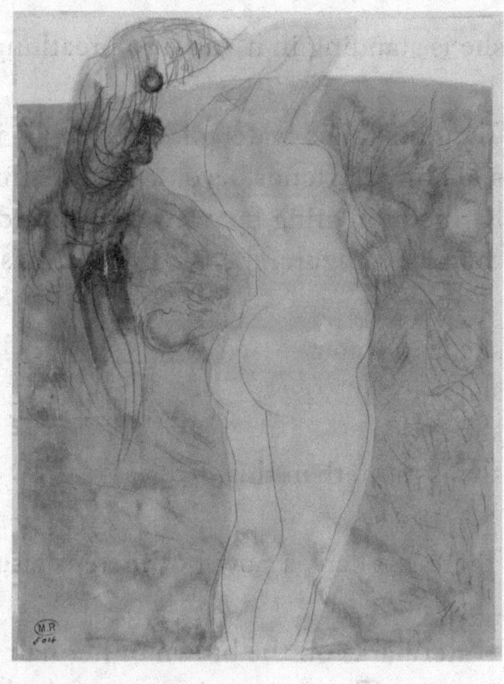

Spring

In *Female Nude in Profile with Loose Hair*, the figure is standing, facing away at a three-quarter angle, exposing her back, buttocks, and backs of her legs.

She is almost completely immersed in blue, but the wash ends a few centimetres from the top of the image, leaving her head, face, and part of her right arm in the skin-toned space of the paper.

Her hands are concealed by her long hair, as though she is washing it, her facial features relaxed, despite the almost chaotic, smudged lines creating them.

This image is very different—there is a oneness with the environment:

she is not struggling
she is not consumed by the water

she is standing in it, but also breathing, existing outside it

The skin-toned watercolour her body is painted with sometimes extends beyond the lines marking the outline of her body, inviting the viewer to consider that she is more than just a figure, she is more than just her body.

she is in water
she is in air
she is this
she is more than this

There is a here, a now, but there is also a beyond, an after.

Watermarks on the brown of her hair form rings of darker pigment. They are on the part of the hair that is in water — all but one: the one on the hair that is out of the water speaks of a kind of merging, an elemental continuity.

Finally, the fact that the drawing of her body begins at the bottom of the page not at her feet, but at the part just above the ankles, creates, within this image of apparent pause and arrival, a gentle, light tension, an almost imperceptible sense of buoyancy:

with no ground in evidence, no sea floor, she could be suspended in water, with a lightness, borne out by her exposed head and arm, so accomplished, she can be seen to have defied gravity.

Untethered by contexts and narratives,

she is in a state of perpetual transition, forever arriving and departing.

she is in a state of '*flow:* to proceed continuously and effortlessly'

Fragment 64

I feel relief, but recovery, it seems, offers little consolation; a cold comfort.

A kind of lightness heavy with the residual weight of pain transformed.

But I can now dare to look at the wound, can tend to it. I can watch it turn into a scar I can live with—a late birthmark.

In a body that is my own again.

Fragment 65

Cicatrix:

the scar of a healed wound

a scar on the bark of a tree

a mark on a stem left after a leaf or other part has become detached

Fragment 66
Temple of Artemis, Vravrona

Spring

This time I have come with offerings—twigs, bones, and feathers I gathered on the island.

The gate is open, the temple no longer floating in water, but on a bed of chamomile and starflower blossom; white, yellow, blue—air, sun, and water transformed.

I find a secluded spot, sit on the ground, and watch as marsh tits fly, swoop, land on the marble columns, perch in the recesses of the ancient structure. Some are curious, flying towards me only to swoop away and return to the temple, looking back as though asking 'what have you come for?'

I sit for a while, happy to watch the birds in this space so different to the lands they left from, wondering at how easily they can make any place their home, even for just a few days, hours sometimes.

When it's time to leave, I lay my gifts amongst the reeds and walk towards the exit, looking back at the birds one last time.

‘I came because I was a young girl once.’

III.

Fragment 67
Antikythera

the moon appeared, full,
as the women stood
around the altar

— Sappho

Fragment 68

I have returned to the island. Here too there was once a temple dedicated to Artemis, but there are no longer any columns, nor architraves, or cornices. Resting amongst the sand and shrubs there is an imprint, a series of the ancient stylobates that formed the basis of the structure.

These blocks of marble are only visible from the track leading down to the beach where they lie, or on moonlit nights, when their white surface reflects the light of the moon.

The moon, her element.

The moon, that sheds a softer, kinder light on the world, on people and their stories.

It is on such a night that I have come to the temple, in late August, and as I sit amongst the ruins, a massive, pearled moon appears from behind the hill on which the windmill stands, illuminating the marble surfaces.

I can hear the sea breathe behind me as the water softly plashes against the pebbles, can feel its salty breath against my skin.

In this space of fragments and silenced stories, in this temple that is no longer here, I feel, finally, at home.

Fragment 69

This time the island feels like a body to me and the more clearly I see it as a body, the more my own begins to feel like an island.

Fragment 70

I think of the underwater channels of icy water that flow into warm rock-pools along the island's coastline and think of my own veins of warm blood, ducts of tears, menstrual blood … *vena*.

You and I are the same,

your ground, my skin, thirsty and dry, warm from the sun, even at dusk, even in the blackest darkness, cooling only in the hours before dawn;

both smelling of thyme.

Shrubs pubic hair, shells nails, wind-bent branches fingers, limbs.
Abandoned houses forsaken lovers, paths journeys, the one and only road the one path back to me.

Caves cavities. Hollows, from *holh*, meaning to cover, to conceal.

The lighthouse, remote, but promising safety.

Fragment 71

When treating patients who have suffered trauma, therapists adopt a 'pendulating' approach, meaning that both therapist and patient will approach the truth gradually, establishing inner 'islands of safety' within the body.[4]

Imagining myself as an island these past few days, I can relate to that and take it further, explore it deeper, on a more internal, visceral level.

I like how the word 'island' is the one I used when describing how I felt, so the harmony of the same choice of word feels healing in my relationship to language.

Fragment 72

It is in the sea that I feel the change

    a softening

in how my body moves with the water

as both breathe

    rise and fall

        merge and dissolve

in one slow, rolling motion

—the sea a whale, blue,

with no end or beginning

Fragment 73

I want to gather all the bones and twigs and feathers and re-build me. From scratch.

hoopoe feathers in my hair
charcoal and earth on my skin
streaks of blood on my face
on the insides of my thighs

I want to walk ankle-deep through sea-washed pebbles until my toenails are polished shells, smooth crescents of moon-crust

feathers in my hair, moon-shell toenails, blood on my skin

Fragment 74

I am submerged, holding a large rock to keep me from surfacing, listening to the silence of the water. It is a still, windless day, the sea surrounding me lambent with dancing pools and rings of light as the sun skims and breaks through the surface. The pools and rings of light, the water, are all silent.

After years of silence, of silent pain, silent shame, I let the rock fall, watch it sink, as I rise to the surface.

Acknowledgements

While only my name appears on the cover, there are many more who played a part in this memoir's completion and deserve the deepest thanks.

First and foremost, my husband Pericles, who is always inspiring and supporting me. It was from Pericles I first learned about the island of Antikythera and it was him I left behind in Athens, alone during what should have been our annual holiday, to discover the island the first time I ever went there.

The island of Antikythera and its people, my home away from home, where I learned that it is possible to feel safe and free.

Eli Navarette, friend and bird whisperer extraordinaire, who took me by the hand and taught me everything I know about birds.

My sister Marina and Christo, my brother-in-law, whose unconditional love and support have been the most precious constant in my life.

My mother and father, who, each in their own way, taught me the beauty and power of language, and my grandmother Lela, who taught me to love art.

Frank Brown, known to some as David Blake, friend and mentor, who took me under his beautiful, eccentric wing and changed my view of the world forever.

Diana Farr Louis, who has been reading my writing ever since I can remember and has always encouraged and supported me.

My poet friends, Emmie Llewelyn, Angela Williams, Pamela Stocker, Joyce Albergine, and Pamela Mordecai, my writing family, who held space for me and this manuscript with generosity and tenderness and a much-needed sharp eye. Their ability to offer constructive criticism with kindness is unparalleled.

Samantha Clark, my mentor, whose invaluable advice helped me transform a clunky first draft and find the right form for my story. I wouldn't have written this memoir without her.

My therapist, Athina Trigeni, who patiently guided me back to the past and helped me find my way back to a very different present.

Sophia Angelis, dear friend, who let me live in her house for much longer than anticipated so I could make a new start when I really needed to.

The team at Vine Leaves Press. Melissa Slayton, my editor, whose invaluable feedback helped me complete what I thought was a finished text. Jessica Bell and Amie

McCracken for offering my memoir a home, and, last but not least, Heather Marshall, the first person at Vine Leaves Press to read the memoir and believe it had a place in the world.

The writers, poets, and artists who inspired me. Homer, Euripides, and Ovid, whose stories taught me about journeys, resilience and transformation. Sappho, whose work taught me that some stories are best told in fewer words. Tony Scherman, whose collection, *The Rape of Leda*, helped me see what I couldn't. Auguste Rodin, whose work gave me the language I needed to describe the indescribable. His drawings, although, perhaps, an unusual choice for a woman recovering from sexual trauma, made me feel closer to my late grandmother who first introduced me to his work, but also allowed me to consider the female body through the lens of the male gaze and find and reclaim what lay beyond. Poet Ocean Vuong, whose observation in an interview that writing is the work of care and that care is anger transformed, helped me move beyond my own anger.

The team at the Antikythera Bird Observatory, for accepting me as a volunteer even though I knew nothing about birds.

Finally, the birds of Antikythera, who showed me how to defy the gravity of my past.

Endnotes

1 Argyro Nafplioti, "The Antikythera Shipwreck," p. 57, Hellenic Ministry of Culture and Tourism, National Archaeological Museum, Kapon Editions, 2012, pp 57-58.
2 Hyginus, *Fabulae*, paragraph 77, https://topostext.org/work/206.
3 https://www.legislation.gov.uk/ukpga/1967/87/section/1
4 Bessel Van der Kolk, *The Body Keeps the Score*, Penguin Books, 2015, p. 245

Fragments 20, 48, and 67 are from the poems of Sappho, rendered by the author from the Greek.

Vine Leaves Press

Enjoyed this book?
Go to *vineleavespress.com* to find more.
Subscribe to our newsletter:

www.ingramcontent.com/pod-product-compliance
Lightning Source LLC
LaVergne TN
LVHW030922080826
845145LV00013B/3019

* 9 7 8 3 9 8 8 3 2 2 1 4 2 *